Ways into Science

Push and Pull

Written by Peter Riley

W
FRANKLIN WATTS
LONDON • SYDNEY

First published in 2001 by Franklin Watts
96 Leonard Street, London EC2A 4XD

Franklin Watts Australia
56 O'Riordan Street
Alexandria, NSW 2015

Series editor: Rachel Cooke
Assistant editor: Adrian Cole
Series design: Jason Anscomb
Design: Michael Leaman Design Partnership
Photography: Ray Moller (unless
otherwise credited)

A CIP catalogue record for this book
is available from the British Library.

ISBN 0 7496 3953 9

Dewey Classification 531

Printed in Malaysia

Picture credits:
John Birdsall Photography p. 6r; Image Bank/
Lars Klove p. 11t

Thanks to our models:
Olivia Al-Adwani, Ammar Duffus, Russell Langer,
Gabrielle Locke, Rukaiyah Qazi, Giselle Quarrington,
Perry Robinson and Matthew Sharp

Contents

When do you push?   6
When do you pull?   7
Push and play   8
More about pulls   10
Strong and weak   12
Splash!   14
Squash and stretch   16
Too strong   18
Springing back   19
Turn and twist   20
Spinning round   22
On the move   24
Using a force   26
Useful words   28
Some answers   29
Index   30
About this book   30

When do you push?

You push
a pram.

You push
a swing.

When do you **pull?**

You pull a brush through your hair.

You pull a book from your bag.

Do you pull or push your socks on?

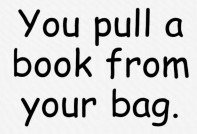

Push and play

A digger pushes rocks into a heap.

A toy car needs a push to make it go.

Michael pushes the keys to play a tune.

Alex pushes the ball when he kicks it.

What pushes and pulls can you find as you play?

An engine
pulls a train.

A tractor pulls
a trailer.

A dog pulls on its lead.

Tim pulls on a jumper.

Can you think of three more pulls?

Strong and weak

Emma gives a weak push to her car.

Ben gives a strong push to his car.

Ben's car goes further than Emma's car.

12

Trevor gives
a weak pull to
the rope.

Aisha gives a strong
pull to the rope.

What do you think will happen?
Turn the page to find out.

Splash!

Aisha pulls Trevor
into the pool.
Trevor gets wet!

Aisha has a stronger
pull than Trevor.

Trevor and Aisha
play again.
This time Trevor
pulls as hard
as Aisha.

What do you
think will
happen?

15

Squash and stretch

A push can squash something.

You push on clay to squash it flat.

A pull can stretch something.

You pull an elastic band to stretch it.

16

Karen squashes a balloon.

What will happen to the balloon?

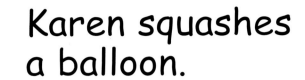

Jessica stretches a lump of clay. What will happen to the clay?

Think about both answers before turning the page to find out what happens.

Too **strong**

The balloon bursts. Karen's push is too strong for the balloon.

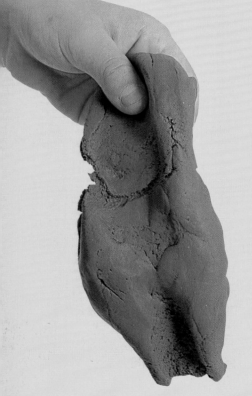

Jessica's pull is too strong for the clay. It breaks into two lumps.

Springing back

When you squash a sponge ball you change its shape. But if you let go the ball springs back into shape.

What happens when you stretch a sock and let it go?

19

You turn this door handle with a push.

Paul pushes the pedals on his bicycle. The wheels turn round.

20

You twist a towel by turning one end round. You hold the other end still – or turn it the other way.

What happens when Emma twists the elastic band of the model aeroplane? See page 22.

Spinning round

The elastic band untwists so the propeller spins round.

Next time, how could Emma make the propeller spin faster?

22

Make this cotton-reel racer.

1. Cut a length of straw a little wider than a cotton reel.

2. Push an elastic band through the straw. Loop it around a small stick at one end.

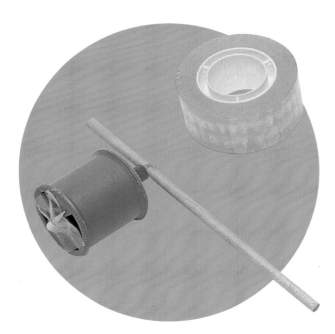

Elastic band

Straw

Small stick

3. Push the straw through the cotton reel.

4. Tape down the small stick. Push a long stick through the other end of the band.

5. Twist the band up tight. Put down your cotton-reel racer and let go!

The pedals on a bicycle turn the wheel so the bicycle moves along.

Paul pushes the pedals harder to move faster.

24

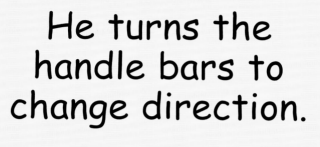

He turns the handle bars to change direction.

He pulls the brakes to go slower.

Should he go faster or slower when he changes direction?

Using a  force

You use a force every time you move something, change its direction or change its shape.

A push is a force (see page 6).

A pull is a force (see page 7).

You use pushing and pulling forces to twist and turn things, too.

Jessica tries to bend some things.

She uses pushing and pulling forces.

She sorts the things into groups.

Try to bend a collection of things. Sort them into groups as well.

Make a table of your results.

Bend	Do not bend
straw	brick
string	screw
ribbon	rock
card	

Useful words

bend - to put a curve in something that is straight by using a force.

direction - When a thing moves from one place to another, it moves in a direction.

engine - a machine which pulls a train or makes a car move.

force - a push or a pull that makes something move, stop moving or change its direction or its shape.

key - the part of a musical instrument you press to make a sound.

propeller - an object on the front of an aeroplane which spins to make the aeroplane move.

pull - a tugging force.

push - a pressing force.

squash - to make something flat by pushing on it.

stretch - to make something long by pulling on it.

turn - to move round in a circle.

twist - to change the shape of something by turning one end.

Some answers

Here are some answers to the questions we have asked in this book. Don't worry if you had some different answers to ours; you may be right, too. Talk through your answers with other people and see if you can explain why they are right.

page 7   You pull your socks on.

page 9   There are lots of different answers to this question. Collect together some toys and see how you make them move to find out the answer for yourself.

page 11   Again there are many answers to this question. Here are just three examples: you can use a pull to open a lid. You pull up a zip to close it. You pull a book off a shelf.

page 15   The pulls are the same so Trevor and Aisha do not move. Nobody gets wet!

page 19   The sock springs back to the length it was before you stretched it.

page 22   Emma could twist the elastic band tighter.

page 25   Paul needs to slow down when he changes direction.

Index

bending 27

direction 25, 26

forces 26, 27

moving 24-25

pull 7, 10-11, 13-15, 16, 18, 20, 25, 26, 27

push 6, 8-9, 12, 16, 18, 20, 24, 26, 27

spinning 22, 23

springy 19

squash 16-18, 19

stretch 16-18, 19

strong 12, 13, 14, 18

turn 20, 24, 25, 26

twist 21-22, 23, 26

weak 12, 13, 14

About this book

Ways into Science is designed to encourage children to begin to think about their everyday world in a scientific way, examining cause and effect through close observation, recording their results and discussing what they have seen. Here are some pointers to gain the maximum use from **Push and Pull**.

• Working through this book will introduce the basic concepts of a force and also some of the language structures and vocabulary associated with it (for example, comparatives such as faster and slower). This will prepare the child for more formal work on forces later in the school curriculum.

• As you read through the book with children, ask them to point to show which way an object moves when it is pushed or pulled. This will prepare them later for the idea that a force works in a particular direction.

• On pages 13, 17 and 21 children are invited to predict the results of a particular action. Ensure you discuss the reason for any answer they give in some depth before turning over the page. Remember, in most situations, our solution is only one of several possibilities. Set up other scenarios for the children to predict and discuss possible outcomes as well.

• Use pages 24/25 to introduce the idea that when things speed up, slow down or change direction, there is a cause (a force).

• To revisit material earlier in the book, make a collection of objects that move and ask the children to establish if they are moved with a push, a pull or either. Discuss with them the best way to record their results.